D0777343

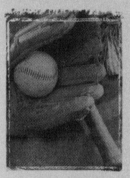

A special gift for my son

_____

With love,

_____

Date

_____

Look for these other *Hugs* books:
Hugs for Coffee Lovers
Hugs for Friends, Book 2
Hugs for Nurses
Hugs for Heroes
Hugs for Women
Hugs for Sisters
Hugs for Grandma
Hugs for Friends
Hugs for Girlfriends
Hugs for New Moms
Hugs for Mom
Hugs for Daughters
Hugs for Grads
Hugs for Kids
Hugs for Teens
Hugs for Teachers
Hugs for Those in Love
Hugs for the Hurting
Hugs for Grandparents
Hugs for Dad
Hugs for Women on the Go
Hugs for the Holidays
Hugs to Encourage and Inspire

Stories, sayings, and Scriptures to Encourage and Inspire

hugs™
for Sons

Debbie Webb

Personalized Scriptures by
LeAnn Weiss

Our purpose at Howard Publishing is to:

- *Increase faith* in the hearts of growing Christians
- *Inspire holiness* in the lives of believers
- *Instill hope* in the hearts of struggling people everywhere

Because He's coming again!

Hugs for Sons © 2003 by Debbie Webb
All rights reserved. Printed in the United States of America
Published by Howard Publishing Co., Inc.
3117 North 7th Street, West Monroe, LA 71291-2227

06 07 08 09 10 11 12   10 9 8 7 6 5

Paraphrased scriptures © 2003 LeAnn Weiss, 3006 Brandywine Dr.,
Orlando, FL 32806; 407-898-4410

Edited by Between the Lines
Interior design by Stephanie Denney

Library of Congress Cataloging-in-Publication Data

Webb, Debbie, 1957–
    Hugs for sons : stories, sayings, and scriptures to encourage and inspire /
Debbie Webb ; personalized scriptures by LeAnn Weiss.
        p. cm.
    ISBN: 1-58229-311-2
        1. Parents—Prayer-books and devotions—English. 2. Sons—Religious
life. I. Weiss, LeAnn. II. Title.

BV4529.W43 2003
242'.642—dc21

                                                        2003050836

Contents

CHAPTER ONE: The "Terrible Twos"............ 1

CHAPTER TWO: Boyhood 19

CHAPTER THREE: Team Player 37

CHAPTER FOUR: Teen Heroes 55

CHAPTER FIVE: Coming of Age 73

CHAPTER SIX: Maturity 89

CHAPTER SEVEN: For Eternity 107

The "Terrible Twos"

I'm compassionate and gracious, slow to anger, and abounding in love for you. I know the hope-filled plans I have for you. I'm at work in you to help you make the right choices, following My good purpose for your life. Even before you were born, I ordained all of your days! Look to Me to keep you occupied with gladness of heart, enjoying what you do.

Patiently,
Your God of Hope

—from Psalm 103:8; Jeremiah 29:11; Philippians 2:13; Psalm 139:16; Ecclesiastes 5:19–20

My son. Those two little words are capable of moving mountains in a mother's life. My son. Two words summoning forth a tidal wave of emotion—a powerful surge of parental love.

My son. The tiny being I carried right under my heart for nine months. I marveled as you made your debut into the world—completely dependent upon my commitment to you, my willingness to care for you, to love you, to help you become the man you were destined to be.

My son. A miniature man dashing through the yard, crushing flowers in your hand—delivering me from piles of laundry, a sink full of dishes, unmade beds, and low-vaulted wishes into an expanse of unbridled affection and uninhibited expression. My son. Causing me to laugh and consoling me when I cry—fearless in the face of make-believe foes, rescuing me from imagined dangers, championing my honor. Still needing my affirmation, my understanding, my appreciation, and my respect.

My son. A man in the making, a heart like putty in my hands. My son. A life so vital, so vibrant, so full of promise, just waiting to take flight, assume your independence, fulfill your calling, make your mark, and express your masculine soul.

My son. God's man. My son.

Childhood is
the world
of miracle
and wonder:
as if creation
rose, bathed in
light out of
the darkness,
utterly new
and fresh
and astonishing.

■

Eugene Ionesco

She bolted down the hall, out the door, and across the street, shuddering at the thought of his crossing the pavement alone.

Leif at Large

Sheila Simmons had had a tough day. So tough that she had considered turning in her "mother badge" temporarily. Life with Leif, the youngest of her four children, was a trying ordeal at times. But this was, without a doubt, one of the most difficult days yet.

Leif was proof, as far as Sheila was concerned, that every shred of stubbornness stored within her DNA had accumulated in her womb and had been deposited in total into this one tiny soul. Leif was the most tenacious little guy she had ever encountered. He was only two years old, yet Sheila found herself doing battle with him every day.

CHAPTER ONE: THE "TERRIBLE TWOS"

That particular morning, Leif and Sheila had gotten an early start on their conflict. Typically, they held off until lunch and then launched into head-to-head combat over whether to eat the "sammich" or the cookie first. But this day was destined for trouble from the beginning.

It began when Leif discovered the knob on the kitchen door and the freedom that awaited him on the other side. Having successfully operated the mechanism once, he persisted in re-opening the door in an attempt to let himself out. Though Sheila kept blocking it, it was of no use. Leif found a way around every barrier.

Sometime around midmorning, Sheila made the mistake of letting down her guard momentarily. An urgent phone call from a friend proved to be a brief but unforgiving distraction.

A sudden silence caused Sheila to drop the receiver onto its cradle and run to the kitchen. Too late! The door had succumbed to Leif's manipulation and was standing wide open. He had escaped. Sheila ran to the carport, face flushed with fear, yelling, "Leif!"

Leif was standing knee-deep in a mud hole just ten steps

away. A bucket was turned upside down on his head. Wet, black soil from inside was dropping in clumps onto his shoulders and down the front of his shirt.

His voice sounded muffled. "Mama!" he said with glee. "I right here. See me!"

She saw him, all right. After spraying him down with the water hose and plopping him into the bathtub, Sheila tried to reason with her baby boy. "Leif," she said patiently but firmly, "you must *not* go outside when Mama is not with you."

"Mama's not wif you," he repeated, grinning impishly.

"No, Leif." She tried again. "Mama *must* be with you when you go outside."

"Leif go outside!" he squealed, splashing the water with his hands.

"Leif, this isn't funny," Sheila scolded as she scrubbed his scalp.

"Leif funny," he grinned, winding her heart a little tighter around his. She hugged him up in a towel, drying him off and struggling to keep everything in perspective. *He's difficult right now,* she thought. *But I'm certain one day his tenacity will prove to be an asset.*

CHAPTER ONE: THE "TERRIBLE TWOS"

Within the next couple of hours, Leif squeezed a tube of toothpaste into Sheila's new leather purse, pulled the cat's whiskers out of one side of its face, smashed his peanut butter sandwich into the fabric of the dining room chair, poured a box of cornflakes into the dog's water bowl, and snipped a lamp cord in two, causing a fuse to blow and shorting out the electricity.

When Sheila found him scrubbing the toilet with her toothbrush, she snatched him up in exasperation and rushed him off to his room for a nap. She was at her wits' end.

"Leif, if I didn't love you so much," Sheila said, tucking him in, "I'd go get a job so I could get away from you for a while."

Leif smiled up at her irresistibly, reaching to initiate a hug. Sheila couldn't resist his tender embrace. He seemed so innocent, causing a tinge of guilt to sting her heart. *How could I get so angry with him?* she asked herself. *He's just little, and he doesn't mean to be so much trouble.*

Thirty minutes later, Sheila's phone rang.

"Hello?" Sheila answered softly, trying not to wake Leif.

"Sheila, it's Wendy," the neighbor from across the street responded.

"Hi, Wendy," she continued in a hushed tone. "What's up?"

"I thought you might like to know that Leif is here."

"What?" Sheila started. "No, Wendy," she argued, "Leif is sound asleep in his room. I laid him down thirty minutes ago, and I haven't heard a peep since."

"Sheila," Wendy scolded mildly, "your son is standing right here."

"I'll be right over!" Sheila exclaimed, slamming down the receiver.

Bursting into Leif's room, Sheila discovered that the window near his bed had been unlocked and opened, and the screen had been removed.

That little rascal! Sheila thought.

She bolted down the hall, out the door, and across the street, shuddering at the thought of his crossing the pavement alone.

Sure enough, there he was, looking above reproach.

"Leif!" Sheila burst into tears. "What is Mommy going to do with you?" She took his face in both her hands and looked intently into his eyes. "Leif," she commanded in her sternest voice, "you must *never* do that again!"

"Mommy cry?" Leif inquired with genuine concern reflected in his furrowed brow. He wiped her tears with his tiny hand.

"Yes, Mommy cry," Sheila sniffed, "because Leif won't mind Mommy."

"Leif mind Mommy!" he beamed, hugging her neck with spontaneous affection.

By the time the rest of the family got home, Sheila was exhausted, frustrated, and weepy. She shared the saga at the supper table, and everyone sat staring at Leif with incriminating looks. They all agreed that Leif should go to bed early. He had worn Sheila completely out, and she needed some peace.

Sheila's husband, Dan, put Leif down for the night, praying aloud at his bedside about obedience. As Dan rejoined the family in the den, he announced, "Everyone relax! Leif is in the bed and the window has been nailed shut." They all giggled. All except Sheila, that is. Her sense of humor was depleted, and exhaustion had taken its place.

A few minutes passed before Leif bellowed from his bedroom, "Mama!" Sheila moved to rise from her seat, but Dan placed his hand on her shoulder to stop her. "Mama!" Leif called again, more pitifully than before.

"Sheila, don't go in there," Dan urged her. "He just needs to go to sleep."

"You're right," she admitted, sighing heavily.

A few more minutes passed before another cry came wafting through the house.

"Daddy!" The pleading in Leif's voice intensified. "Daddy!" he repeated.

"No one move," Dan advised. "He'll give it up pretty soon."

"Don't count on it," Sheila predicted.

Minutes ticked by. Everyone sat silently, waiting for Leif's next move.

He did not disappoint them. "Sarah!" he cried out for his only sister. "Sarah!" Twice he called each name as if in a cadence.

Sarah looked longingly at Dan. "Daddy, can't I go sing to him or something?" she inquired.

"No, sweetheart," Dan responded. "It will simply prolong the contest. Let's hunker down and wait it out. I think we can win this thing."

"Alan!" he tried next. Leif's oldest brother grinned as he waited for the second shout. "Alan!" Leif delivered.

Everyone exchanged looks, the children muffling giggles behind cupped hands.

"Aaron!" Leif howled. This was his last resort. As his youngest sibling, Aaron was the final family member on the roll. "Aaron!" he called.

Confident now that he had exhausted his resources, the family hoped Leif might go to sleep. They had resisted the urge to run to his rescue.

Suddenly… "J-E-E-E-SUS!" Leif bellowed at the top of his lungs, drawing the name out in exaggerated syllables like a TV evangelist during a full-blown revival.

"Can you believe this?" Sheila exclaimed in a whisper. "Only Leif would resort to such extremes—crying out to the Lord as if *He* would come get him."

Dan and Sheila looked at each other, anticipating the second call, but the cadence had stopped—abruptly. Leif had fallen silent. They shifted uncomfortably in their seats.

"What if something's wrong?" Alan whispered, his face reflecting concern.

Leif at Large

At that, the entire family jumped to their feet, and with panic etched on their faces, they ran down the hall and burst into Leif's bedroom together.

There he lay, sound asleep, looking like a cherub.

"That little rascal!" Dan whispered.

"Is that a smile twitching at the corners of his mouth?" Sheila asked, gently tucking him in tighter.

"I'm afraid it is," Dan observed. "He must have known he kept us on edge till the bitter end."

Sheila's heart swelled with love. The day was over, and Leif was finally asleep. It had been a trying day—very difficult indeed. But she was certain as she stood admiring his precious face that it would all pay off.

Leaning over him, she kissed him and thanked the Lord silently for resisting his cry for deliverance. Leif was a gift to her grateful heart.

CHAPTER TWO

Boyhood

Listening to your earthly parents results in grace and honor. Remember My teachings by keeping My commands in your heart, and I'll give you longer life and prosperity. Don't rely on your own limited picture of your situation. When you trust in Me wholeheartedly and make Me your top priority in all that you do and say, I'll keep your life on track.

Guiding you,
Your Wonderful Counselor and Mighty God

—from Proverbs 1:8–9; 3:1–2, 5–6; Isaiah 9:6

As parents we imagine that we are equipping you with the tools you will need in order to survive. We conjure up noble ideals we think we are capable of modeling. And with great diligence, we teach you our values: faith, hope, love, compassion, honesty, loyalty, courage, dependability, and the like. We glorify our standards—our image of ourselves, though merely reflecting the ordinary—and esteem ourselves mentors worthy of regard. Then suddenly, the tables turn on us, and we realize we are the ones being taught.

Sons become men in the most unexpected circumstances, at the most unanticipated moments. Perhaps in a season of trouble or distress, a boy rises to the occasion, responding to an urgent need or a cry of desperation. Or a quiet moment of rest and reprieve may inspire the sagacious comment of a young man coming into his own. Whatever the case, we parents are stunned by the wisdom, good judgment, and understanding you voice.

We realize in times like these that all along an Unseen Hand has assisted us in our job. Another loving Parent has taken your learning even further than we knew, directing your heart in a bent more profound than we had known—one far nobler than our own.

Nothing is more humbling than this dawning awareness that our little boy's body houses the independent spirit of a man—a man wiser and more faithful to our values than we had esteemed ourselves capable of being. And we are grateful that we are not in control after all.

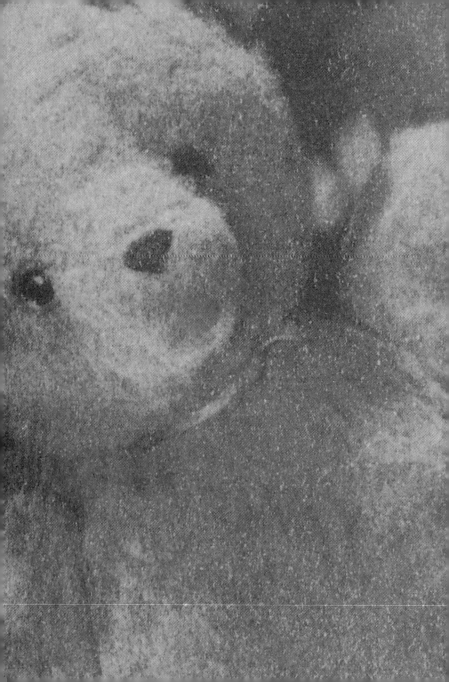

Oh, what a mighty influence home life has on us! Indeed, we do not know how deep a debt we owe to our mothers and fathers and their training.

■

Oswald Chambers

*An hour later, there was still
no sign of the boys.
Renee was beside herself.
"My baby!" she wailed
in Sam's arms.
"You've lost my baby!"*

Lost and Found

"Renee, I didn't realize moving to the city would be so hard on you," Sam said to his wife one morning while reading his newspaper. "I'm really sorry."

"I'll be fine, Sam," Renee responded. "It will simply take some time. We're having to unlearn lifelong habits associated with living in a small community, and it's frightening to me—not to mention just plain, hard work."

Sam's conscience stung with a twinge of guilt. Moving to St. Louis was his idea, but he had been confident that it was the best thing for his family.

"Honey, the world's not a safe place anymore," Sam

responded. "Our kids need to learn that you can't go through life trusting strangers and exploring unfamiliar neighborhoods for the sake of adventure."

"I know," Renee responded. "It's just a little overwhelming, that's all."

Renee hadn't wanted to make this move. The big city intimidated her. "The question that haunts me is," she continued, "do our children stand a better chance of learning our values in a small town, surrounded by familiar faces?"

Sam returned to reading his newspaper, wrestling internally with Renee's question.

Though she was not consoled, Renee was ready to move on. Her older sister and brother-in-law, Shelby and Mitch, were coming with their children to spend the weekend. Renee would spend the day preparing for their guests.

On Saturday morning, Shelby and Renee were up early, bustling about. They had made plans for an enjoyable excursion at a nearby park with plenty of playground equipment, miles of hiking trails, and acres of trees.

"Mama!" Ben exclaimed as he ran into the kitchen.

Lost and Found

Renee greeted him with a hug and lots of kisses. "How's my baby this morning?" she asked.

"Jimmy and me are going hunting!" Ben responded enthusiastically.

Jimmy was Ben's older cousin.

"Hunting for what?" Renee inquired.

"For bears!" Ben exclaimed.

"Well, we *are* going to Castleton Park, son, but I'm not sure you can hunt bears there," Renee advised.

"We can, Mama," Ben assured her. "I know we can."

■

Other than a bee sting, an overripe watermelon, and a relentless splinter in the heel of Jimmy's hand, the day went well. They played ball, rode bicycles, had a water-balloon fight, and finally sat down to a delicious picnic lunch.

After lunch Sam announced, "All the guys are hiking the trail back to the car. You girls can either go with us or take the shortcut back."

"We need to finish cleaning up," Renee told Sam, waving them on. "We'll meet you at the parking lot in forty-five minutes."

CHAPTER TWO: BOYHOOD

When the girls strode up the sidewalk toward the car, they found the men had arrived ahead of them. Renee's eyes scanned the group. Someone was missing.

"Where's Ben?" she yelled to Sam from a distance.

"What do you mean, where's Ben?" Sam yelled in response.

Renee quickened her pace. "I mean, *where's Ben?*" Renee demanded curtly.

"He's supposed to be with you," Sam said defensively.

"No," Renee accused, "he's supposed to be with you! It was a boy/girl thing, remember?"

Shelby approached then, looking confused. "Where's Jimmy?" she inquired.

"Ben and Jimmy didn't want to finish the hike," Sam started to explain, "so we let them follow the trail back to where you were."

"Sam Jamison!" Renee exploded. "What were you thinking? You weren't supposed to let them leave you."

Sam knew he was guilty, yet he continued defensively: "Well, now that we've established *blame*, Renee, why don't we get busy trying to find the boys."

Outraged, Renee shot an incriminating look at Sam,

Lost and Found

grabbed Shelby by the wrist, and stomped off toward the picnic site. Everyone else followed, and the search began.

"Sam, it's been an hour since we started looking. I'm starting to panic," Renee said, tears welling up in her eyes.

"I think we need to divide up so we can cover more ground," Sam suggested. "Let's comb through these woods and meet in that clearing on the other side."

"Ben! Jimmy! Where are you?" The small search party could hear each other calling from every direction.

"I can't help picturing my little Ben wandering around out here, scared and lost," Renee sobbed to her sister.

"Renee," Shelby tried to sound confident, "Jimmy is four years older; he will take care of Ben."

When they met in the open meadow, Sam's face was etched with worry. "Let's make one more pass through that section of woods on the other side of the parking lot," he suggested.

An hour later, there was still no sign of the boys. Renee was beside herself. "My baby!" she wailed in Sam's arms. "You've lost my baby!"

"I think we'd better call the police," Mitch said grimly. "It's starting to get dark."

They loaded into the minivan, reluctant to drive away but feeling out of options.

As Sam turned out of the gate, a red compact car with a pizzeria sign on top drove right up behind them and honked. The young man driving appeared animated—upset. Sam waved him off and kept moving. The car honked again, this time more persistently, and the young man waved his arm from the driver's window.

"What's his problem?" Sam exclaimed. "I didn't pull out in front of him. He sped up."

The horn continued to bellow, and the car's lights started flashing. "Oh, for heaven's sake!" Sam said as he pulled over out of exasperation. "I've got to get this guy off our tail, or we'll never get anywhere."

Sam edged onto the shoulder. The red car pulled over behind him.

Sam opened his door, preparing to argue. As he started toward the car, the back doors flew open, and out jumped Ben and Jimmy!

"Mom!" Jimmy yelled. "It's me!"

Everyone jumped out and ran into a huddle, crying,

laughing, and hugging. Renee had Ben in a vice grip, planting kisses all over his face.

Ben appeared completely composed and unaffected by the whole event. He just stood there smiling, waiting for the tide of emotion to pass.

"What happened to you?" Sam asked.

"Me and Jimmy went hunting for bears, Dad," Ben explained, confident that everyone would understand.

"But you were supposed to go straight back to your mother," Sam scolded. "Do you know how worried we've been?"

"We did go straight back, Dad," Ben countered. "But we went through the woods instead of on the trail."

"But you got lost," Renee interjected.

"We got lost because Jimmy said we needed to turn right," Ben continued. "I knew he was wrong, but he wouldn't listen."

Mitch looked at Jimmy, now blushing from embarrassment. "Jimmy, what were you thinking?" Mitch confronted gently.

"I don't know," Jimmy mumbled as he kicked the dirt with his toe.

CHAPTER TWO: BOYHOOD

"Well, tell us, then," Mitch insisted. "How did you end up with the pizza guy?"

"We walked for what seemed like a whole day," Jimmy explained. "We hollered and hollered until we got hoarse and couldn't holler anymore. The sun was starting to set, and I was getting pretty scared, thinking we were never going to find you guys before dark. I screamed at Ben, 'What are we gonna do?'"

Jimmy paused. Looking up into his father's face, he said quietly, "Dad, you won't believe what happened."

"Yes, I will, son," Mitch consoled. "Go ahead and tell us."

"Well, Ben grabbed hold of me and said, 'I think we need to stop wasting our time looking and just pray, Jimmy.'" He paused again, then finished his story somewhat reverently. "Ben got down on his knees and looked up into the sky with his eyes wide open, and he prayed real simple-like. He said, 'Lord, I know You can see that we're lost. Could You help us out a little, here? Thanks, Lord. Amen.'"

"When he finished," Jimmy continued, "he got up and pointed his finger. 'We're going that way,' he said. And we did. We found a road, and the pizza guy drove straight up to us, as if he knew he was supposed to, and stopped. We told him the situation, and he brought us here."

Everyone stood silent, staring at Ben.

Renee broke the silence as she took Ben's face in her hands. "I'm so proud of you, son," she said, tears sparkling in her eyes.

"Why, Mama?" Ben asked.

"Because you knew to pray," Renee responded, kissing his cheek.

"Didn't you know to pray, Mama?" Ben inquired.

"I guess I didn't," Renee answered, taken a little off guard. "I was just afraid."

"Afraid of what?" Ben asked.

"Afraid of not finding you," Renee continued. "Afraid that you were afraid. I just get really scared sometimes."

"But why, Mama?" Ben pressed.

"I guess because I don't feel safe in this big city like I did before we moved," Renee answered honestly.

"But Mama, you told me God was coming with us. Well, you were right. He did!"

"You're right, Ben," Renee answered, finally feeling at peace about their new home. "He did."

CHAPTER THREE

Team Player

Remember, I'm on your team. You can do all things because I strengthen you. Don't just focus on yourself; also consider the interests and needs of others. When you have a servant's heart, you're great by My standards. May your light shine before people so that they'll see your good deeds and praise Me.

Cheering you on,
Your God of Encouragement

—from Romans 8:31; Philippians 4:13; 2:4;
Matthew 20:26–27; 5:16

Parenthood is by far the most intriguing and challenging job of all. It's more than I bargained for when I first considered having a child. I marveled as a tiny bundle of life emerged by miraculous delivery and then watched with awe as you developed into a man of strength and integrity. The process surpassed both my understanding and my capabilities. You became who you are by the grace of God, in spite of the interference of my meager attempts.

I've watched in absolute wonder as you've progressed from a curious toddler to a confident and competent team player. I've seen you develop from a teetering preschooler, fumbling to tie your shoes, to a consummate professional, capable of handling the most arduous tasks. I've seen you step from the mudholes in our yard to the mountaintops of spiritual achievement. I've stood witness as your character matured from the innocence of youth into the strength and resilience of manhood.

I tried to instill in you the values I hold dear, to teach you the principles I believed would make you a better man. I thought I was holding before you the highest standards. But you surpassed my expectations. In the moment of trial, you triumphed. In the face of adversity, you overcame. When the real test of character confronted you, you passed with flying colors. You are the son I always hoped you'd be…and more.

Caring is
a powerful
force.

■

Frank Reed

Johnson couldn't do anything related to baseball. The question on everyone's mind was, Why is Johnson out here?

Johnson!

His nickname was "The Gun." Jake could throw a baseball from deep center field to home plate on a dime, with nearly no arch. His strength and precision in the outfield set him apart early on. And Jake was fast—very fast.

"Those college scouts have their eye on you," Coach Donahue told Jake. "It isn't often they see talent like yours. You need to stay focused, son, and don't let it go to your head."

Jake's father, Tim, was his biggest fan. Tim never missed a game. He arranged his schedule around practices, took vacation for tournaments, and skipped meals to attend games. A boy couldn't ask for a more devoted fan and father.

But as a parent, Tim shared the coach's concern. "Through the years," he told Jake, "I've witnessed the downfall of many young athletes who forgot that it takes a whole team to win the pennant."

"I hear ya, Dad," Jake said, hoping to avoid a sermon.

"I just don't want that to happen to you, son," Tim persisted. "Never lose sight of the value of others."

"I won't, Dad," Jake assured him. "I promise." Tim made a mental note to resume the discussion at a more opportune time.

Midseason, Jake was put on athletic probation because of a poor grade in Algebra. He wouldn't be allowed to finish the season.

"Son, this is the worst thing you could have done!" Tim fumed.

"I know, Dad," Jake responded defensively. "But my spot on the summer roster is secure, and that's the most critical season."

"So how are you going to stay in shape?"

Johnson!

"I'm going to join the spring city league," Jake responded.

"It's been seven years since you've played on a city team!" Tim exclaimed. "Your skill level is way beyond those guys."

"It takes a whole team to win the pennant, Dad," Jake reminded him.

■

Soon after joining his new team, Jake realized he'd forgotten what it was like to play "down." Tim sensed Jake's frustration over the frequent errors and noticed him shaking his head from time to time in the outfield. His concern deepened. Could Jake still relate to being one of the guys?

Among all the mediocre performers on the city team, one stood out. He was as *incapable* of playing baseball as Jake was *capable*: Sean Johnson.

Johnson had red hair, slicked back like someone out of the 1950s. He was gangly and lagged behind in his physical development. Bunched up around his waist, his pants were tucked into his belt in an awkward manner, contributing to an overall unathletic appearance.

CHAPTER THREE: TEAM PLAYER

Johnson couldn't do anything related to baseball—throw, catch, hit, or run. The question on everyone's mind was, *Why is Johnson out here?*

One day during practice, the ball was popped up to Johnson in right field. He ducked down, covering his head with his glove and squatting on the ground, letting the ball bounce and roll into foul territory. The coach yelled, "Johnson, do you want to play baseball or not?"

Upon returning to the dugout, Johnson said, "Coach, I *don't* want to play baseball. My parents are *making* me play. Just let me sit on the bench from now on, OK?"

Jake overheard the conversation and felt like someone had punched him in the gut. Why would his parents force him to play baseball? Anyone could see that Johnson wasn't cut out for sports.

From then on, the coach did leave Johnson on the bench. Game after game, the coach passed over him when someone came off the field. Johnson just sat with his head down.

One night, in the bottom of the sixth inning with two outs, the batter tripped on his way to the plate, twisting his ankle. He crumpled to the ground, then limped off, too hurt

Johnson!

to play. Jake had an idea. He stood up, then approached the dugout fence. "Johnson!" he yelled at the third base coach.

Every head in the dugout snapped to attention. Coach Smith looked at Jake, confused. Jake yelled again, "Johnson! Johnson!"

At that, Coach Smith signaled Jake to sit down. Jake shook the fence, causing it to rattle loudly and yelled again, "Johnson! Johnson!"

Suddenly, the catcher got up from the bench in support of Jake's petition. Grabbing the fence, he added his voice to Jake's: "Johnson! Johnson!"

Jake motioned the rest of his teammates to join them. One by one, every member of the team stood up at the fence and joined the chorus. "Johnson! Johnson!"

The coach shook his head in resignation and yelled, "Johnson, it's all up to you, son!"

Johnson's face was flushed. A mixture of anxiety and excitement filled his eyes. Jake grabbed him by the shirt and slapped him on the back to encourage him. Johnson emerged from the dugout, bat in hand, while the whole team chanted, "Johnson! Johnson!"

CHAPTER THREE: TEAM PLAYER

"Strike one!" the umpire yelled as the ball passed over the plate.

The team kept cheering. "Johnson! Johnson!"

"Strike two!" the ump screamed with puffy cheeks. Johnson looked back at his parents. They were standing on the bleachers.

"Strike three! You're out!" the ump bellowed, motioning as though he were jerking the final ball right out of the dirt.

Johnson turned toward the dugout. He looked surprised to find the team cheering him wildly in spite of his dismal performance. Jake headed out of the dugout with Johnson's glove, greeting him as though he'd hit a home run. Cheering, rubbing his head, and slapping his backside, the team followed Jake's lead in giving Johnson high fives. "Way to hang, dude," they praised him. "You were on him." "Next time, buddy."

Three outs later, the game was over and Johnson had participated in a win.

While Johnson's parents cheered with the rest, Tim sat quietly, contemplating the event. He was proud that the young renegade who had caused the unconventional ruckus was his son.

Johnson!

From then on, Jake called for Johnson in every game. Coach Smith went along, thankful for the support of his team. And though Johnson's playing skills weren't improving much, his self-esteem was. He became a part of the team, and his spirits were soaring.

But Jake's truest colors were revealed in the final game of the season. Thanks in large part to Jake's exceptional skill, the team had a shot at the play-offs for the first time in years. Now, with the score tied and two outs, Jake had hit the ball deep into right field—a triple. He landed square on the base and held his fist in the air, signaling a time out. Coach Smith walked over. Tim could see Jake pointing at his ankle and limping around the base.

Jake motioned toward the dugout; the coach shook his head emphatically. Jake took a step closer and said something else to the coach.

Coach Smith appeared distressed. He removed his hat, scratched the top of his head, and waved toward the dugout. "Johnson, get out here and pinch-run for 'The Gun.'"

Jake grinned with satisfaction and headed back to the dugout, signaling a thumbs-up at Johnson as they crossed paths. He found his place at the fence among the other team members waiting for the base hit he hoped was coming.

"Dude," the catcher confronted Jake, "you're not hurt—you sprinted back in."

"Don't worry about it," Jake responded. "I know what I'm doing."

"Why would you give it away like that?" he persisted.

"I said don't worry about it," Jake scolded. "I'll have other chances like this, but this could be Johnson's only shot."

Crack! The bat connected—a line drive into left field. Johnson wasn't sure what to do. Could he make it home? Jake was certain of one thing—this might be Johnson's only opportunity. "Run, Johnson!" he yelled. "Run with all you've got!"

Johnson looked at Jake and started running—unsure of himself, but still running. Jake yelled louder. "Run harder, Johnson. Run like your pants are on fire!"

Johnson picked up some speed. The left fielder had the ball. He reared back to throw it home. Jake yelled, "Slide, Johnson! Slide!"

Johnson!

Johnson slid. Or tripped. No one really knew. But somehow, Johnson made it home before the ball did, tumbling over the plate and into the catcher. Game over. Johnson had scored the winning run!

Jake led the charge out of the dugout, cheering. The team lifted Johnson onto their shoulders and walked around the infield chanting, "Johnson! Johnson!"

Johnson's parents were on their feet in the stands, cheering wildly. Johnson basked in his moment of glory, grinning from ear to ear.

Tim stood in the bleachers with tears in his eyes. Every concern had been put to rest. His son had had the chance to be the star of the game—of the season, of the league—but he gave it all up for someone who *really* needed to shine—someone whose life would forever be changed by scoring the winning run that day.

CHAPTER FOUR

Teen Heroes

I am your refuge and your strength. I'm always here to help, no matter what challenge you face. Watch Me make all grace overflow to you, so that you'll always have all that you need to excel in every good work. May you act justly, love mercy, and walk humbly by My side.

Victoriously,
Your Dependable God

—from Psalm 46:1; 2 Corinthians 9:8; Micah 6:8

What do parents hope their sons will become when they grow up? Doctors, lawyers, coaches, teachers, businessmen, or soldiers?

Soldiers? No!

Soldiers die.

Someone once said, "Mothers should negotiate between nations. Mothers would put a stop to the fighting."

We all hope to inspire patriotism within our sons. We want you to be noble, courageous, loyal, and diligent. We hope to instill in you an integrity that runs miles deep. We want you to be fearless leaders, unstoppable champions, and disciplined citizens. We want you to rise to the top, reach all the goals we fell short of, and champion every cause—but we don't want you risking your life. Not now, not ever.

We hope for heroes, but within limits. We applaud those who wear medals, but from a distance. We offer our opinions about foreign affairs, about peace and war; but we don't offer our sons.

Mothers cry when our young, idealistic sons march off to war. Parents pray desperately when fearless champions of freedom who have their father's eyes and bear their family's name take up arms.

Though we train you to be patriotic, we desperately hope you do not become patriots. But you do it anyway. You rise above fear and cowardice, and in spite of our own lack of courage, you champion dreams.

Great occasions
do not make
heroes or
cowards;
they simply
unveil them
to the eyes
of men…
Crisis shows us
what we have
become.

■

Bishop Westcott

*She had suddenly
realized that there was something extraordinary about her
son's patriotism. As his mother,
she must dignify that.*

Star-Spangled Son

"Steve," Becky said to her husband, "do you ever worry about how obsessed Doug seems with the Gulf War?"

Becky was keenly aware of her son's idealism, especially as it related to patriotism and the never-ending fight for freedom.

"What's to worry about?" Steve responded. "Every boy dreams of being a soldier—a hero."

"But Doug is so impressionable," Becky persisted. "What if he gets so enthralled with the war that he decides to enlist in the armed services?"

"Nonsense, Beck," Steve scolded. "You're worrying about things that just won't happen."

"But what if it did?" she pressed.

"Well, if it did, we'd have a soldier for a son," he answered. "And that's nothing to be ashamed of."

"It isn't shame I'm concerned about," Becky shot back. "It's his courage that scares me."

Becky wanted to believe that Steve was right—that Doug would never join the military. But Becky knew her son, and her heart had been filled with apprehension ever since the accident.

As a freshman in high school, Doug—an accomplished athlete, a leader in his church youth group, and the apple of his mother's eye—had his life mapped out. But life has a way of changing course, sometimes without warning. Such was the case the night Steve and Becky went out to dinner and left Doug at home with a friend.

Doug had always had a zest for adventure. When his friend suggested going sledding on ice, Doug jumped at the chance. He flew down a steep incline at an incredible rate of speed and hit a sapling just big enough to snap his thigh cleanly in two.

Star-Spangled Son

"You'll be flat on your back for six weeks," the physician announced as he finished sculpting Doug's cast. It stretched from the bottom of Doug's foot all the way to his hip.

"Will I need crutches to get around?" Doug inquired.

"You won't be getting around," the doctor informed him. "This is a very difficult bone to set. You'll be confined to bed for six weeks."

Doug's hockey career came to an abrupt end. He quickly fell behind in his schoolwork and out of touch with his friends. Finally his appetite diminished, and so did his strength.

Becky's heart broke for her son. "Steve," she commented one morning, "it seems unfair that the consequences of a simple sledding mishap are so severe. I'm moving the television into his room today, and the whole family can camp out in there with him at night, so we can still be together."

Each day Becky busied herself with things she could do at Doug's bedside. She hardly left him alone. Though she regretted the accident, she cherished the opportunity to have him at home. They spent hours talking and laughing. Their relationship grew closer over the weeks of convalescence.

But something else had grown in Doug's heart while he recuperated, and that's what was worrying Becky. Desert Storm was heating up, and as a temporary invalid, Doug was a captive audience. Becky noticed his fascination with the war right away. Doug's news watching became the seedbed for a new obsession with patriotism, war strategies, and the men who went to war.

One intrepid warrior had captured Doug's attention: five-star General Norman Schwarzkopf of the United States Army. "Stormin' Norman" became Doug's hero. This distinguished man of valor inspired the young idealist lying flat on his back. But no one in Doug's family fully realized with what intensity the young patriot's passion burned. No one, except Becky.

"Son," she ventured one day, "you're fascinated with this war, aren't you?"

"Sure, Mom," Doug replied. "Who wouldn't be? This is history in the making. Those men and women are influencing the future of millions of people, the destiny of nations."

Becky knew her son. She observed the glimmer in his eyes as he watched the war play itself out. She could sense the fervor within him, the soldier gaining ground. As she found herself plagued with a nagging fear, Becky began to pray about the situation.

Two years passed. Becky assumed that the patriot's dream had lessened with the passing of time. Her anxiety slowly dissipated, and life resumed its routine.

One summer, Becky accompanied Doug and the church youth group on a missionary trip to Jamaica. After boarding their connecting flight in Miami, Doug settled into seat 28B near the back of the large jet among his teenage friends. Becky was seated twelve rows up, with two other adult chaperones.

Suddenly, Doug appeared at Becky's elbow, wide-eyed and breathless, tugging at her sleeve: "Mom, quick, give me a pen and a piece of paper—General Schwarzkopf just boarded this plane!"

"What?" Becky exclaimed. "Where?"

"Up in first class," Doug responded. "Come on, Mom, hurry!"

"Son, I'm sure you're mistaken," Becky responded, straining to see. "That can't be him."

CHAPTER FOUR: TEEN HEROES

"What do you mean?" Doug said impatiently. "Mom, I know General Schwarzkopf when I see him. He's my hero!" He grabbed Becky's purse to find a pen. "I've got to get his autograph, Mom. I'll never have this opportunity again."

Finding a pen and some paper, he rushed up the aisle. Becky watched as a man in camouflage responded to Doug's obvious respect and admiration. The older man's arm went around Doug's shoulder, and the instant camaraderie made it appear as if they had known each other for years. By the time Doug rose to return to his seat, the aisle was jammed with passengers who had also caught on and were waiting their turn for the general's autograph.

Doug worked his way back to Becky's seat. Squatting down beside her, his eyes beaming with excitement, he said, "Mom, he's everything I ever thought he would be. He's awesome!"

A few minutes passed, and the flight attendant announced that all passengers must return to their seats. The interior of the plane fell quiet as the jet rumbled down the runway.

Suddenly, a voice broke through the silence. A voice singing. Becky recognized it immediately—it was her son.

Star-Spangled Son

"O say, can you see, by the dawn's early light, What so proudly we hail'd at the twilight's last gleaming?"

At first people looked around, incredulous. No one could believe what they were hearing—a teenage boy back in 28B was singing—solo.

"Whose broad stripes and bright stars, thro' the perilous fight, O'er the ramparts we watch'd, were so gallantly streaming?"

The national anthem, no less.

"And the rockets' red glare, the bombs bursting in air, Gave proof thro' the night that our flag was still there…"

His voice grew stronger; the emotion in his singing was gaining momentum.

"O say, does that star-spangled banner yet wave O'er the land of the free-e-e-e-e…"

He held the note steady and strong. Every passenger was listening, and every face reflected some kind of response. Tears. Smiles. Nodding assent.

"…and the home of the brave?"

Doug finished strong, then smiled shyly at his audience.

The airborne passengers burst into applause. What had been a silent cabin full of strangers was now a cheering band of compatriots. One young man had called them all to a sacred and solemn salute to a statesman of unusual bravery and uncommon strength. Doug had stepped above the status quo and expressed his patriotic devotion in a courageous outburst of spirit and song.

Becky's cheeks were streaked with tears. She looked at the face of her son: His intense, blue eyes brimmed with compassion; his well-defined jaw outlined a maturing masculinity; his ruddy complexion radiated with health and energy. Becky had always loved her son, but new admiration and respect flooded her heart.

"I guess General Schwarzkopf is Doug's hero?" one of the chaperones asked.

"Yes, he is!" she answered with pride. It had been a clarifying moment for Becky. As Doug was singing she had suddenly realized that there was something extraordinary about her son's patriotism, his courage, and his strength of spirit. She realized that, as his mother, she must dignify that.

"Yes, that soldier sitting in first class is my son's hero," Becky said, "but my hero is the boy sitting in 28B, singing solo."

Star-Spangled Son

Three years later, Doug joined the U.S. Marines. *If it hadn't been for that broken leg,* Becky thought as he set off on his first assignment, *this might never have happened.* But Becky knew deep down that a man must do what his heart leads him to do. He must become what he is called to be. And civilian or soldier, Doug would always be her son. Her hero.

CHAPTER FIVE

Coming of Age

Through My divine power, I've blessed you with everything you need for life and godliness. Continually grow in goodness, knowledge, self-control, perseverance, godliness, brotherly kindness, and love. Adding these qualities to your faith will keep you effective and productive in the things that count for eternity.

Graciously,
Your Faithful God

—from 2 Peter 1:3, 5–9

When I stop to consider it, I've noticed that life is comprised of really big things—and then again, just as significantly, of really little things. The big things stand out in your memory, jutting up like monuments that mark your journey with joy or with heartache. But little things pour into all the extra spaces and empty places like finely ground sand—filling in the cracks and buffering the shockwaves of trauma and loss.

You, my son, have contributed significantly to both the big things and the little things in my life. Your remarkable strength and fortitude have come through in times of adversity; your joy and exuberance have energized the best of times. But your consistency and dependability seep into my existence almost without notice, stabilizing the atmosphere and blessing me quietly. You have been there, diligently fulfilling your role in our family as a faithful and irreplaceable part of the whole.

What would my life have been like without you? Void of the blessing your presence has brought; stark and silent where your familiar voice has sounded; incomplete where your inimitable spirit and handsome face have graced our family's home.

Your tender compassion, your gentle strength, your vulnerability and openness are things I have come to depend on daily. What would I have done all these years without you? In a world that otherwise would surely be dull, empty, and lifeless, you are a bright and shining light for my heart.

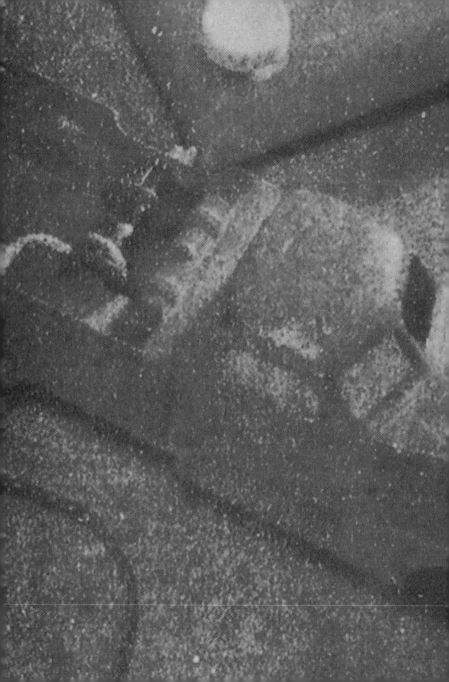

Love leaves
a legacy. How
you treated other
people, not your
wealth or
accomplishments,
is the most
enduring impact
you can leave
on earth.

■

Rick Warren

"Mom, this is the least
I can do after all those
years when you tended to
me in the middle of the
night. Now go to sleep."

The Heart of the Man

"Mom," Caleb said, brow furrowed, as he opened the refrigerator and reached for the orange juice.

Whatever's on his mind, Missy thought to herself, *it's obviously important*. Caleb wasn't the talkative type—at least not in the morning. He preferred to wait until later in the day after his first two classes at the university were behind him.

He shook the jug and unscrewed the cap. "I *really* don't want you sleeping on the couch like you did last night."

Missy smiled, "Well, son, it's sweet of you to be so concerned."

"Mom, I'm not kidding," Caleb scolded, putting the juice container on the counter and turning to look at his mother. "It's not funny. Nobody wants his mom sleeping on the couch. It just isn't right."

"I'm sorry, Caleb, I didn't mean to make light of your concern," she said reassuringly. "I just couldn't rest because your dad was snoring. I won't make a habit of it, I promise."

"No, Mom, I'm talking *never!*" Caleb argued mildly, pouring the juice into his glass. "If Dad's snoring keeps you awake, you can get in my bed, and I'll sleep on the couch. I sleep fine on the couch."

"OK, babe," Missy promised jokingly. "I'll let you suffer from now on."

"Very funny, Mom," he mumbled under his breath. "This isn't a joking matter. You work hard, and you need your rest. You're not getting any younger, you know."

"Hey!" she teased, poking his sides with her fingers, trying to humor him. "Who do you think you are?"

He shrugged off the teasing, and she watched as his tall, muscular frame passed through the kitchen and disappeared through the doorway. The familiar feelings of love and pride welled up in her heart, and she choked back tears. Caleb would be getting married in the next couple of months, and things would just never be the same.

Caleb was the only child out of Missy's brood who had never left home. The fourth of five, Caleb was a conscientious son who opted to attend a local university to cut expenses. Mike and Missy paid for half of their children's education, leaving the other half as their individual responsibility, and Caleb didn't want to graduate with debt.

Missy couldn't have been happier about his decision to stay home. As far as she was concerned, life was just sweeter with him around. Caleb had a cushioning effect on her life. His tender heart and thoughtful ways softened things like a buffer. Missy wasn't ready for him to leave, even at twenty-two. But then, Missy would never be ready.

Where have the years gone? she wondered to herself. Missy had been keenly aware of his extra-tender heart from the beginning. It was the little things that gave him away: the way he catered to his sister or accommodated his younger brother; the way he sensed and responded to his mother's heartache in troubled times; the way he prayed and cared for helpless creatures.

She remembered the time he had discovered a baby bird

that had fallen from its nest. Caleb bounded through the door, yelling, "Mom, come quick! I need you!" Out he ran again, slamming the screen door behind him. Missy thought for certain that someone must be hurt. She ran out behind him and, within a few hurried steps, came to a complete stop. There he was, squatting, hands cupped carefully together, holding something he was studying intently. His big brown eyes, wide with concern, looked up at her as he pleaded, "What should we do, Mom?"

"Let's leave him here and see if his mama will come get him," Missy had suggested.

Caleb looked shocked and hurt. "He'll die!" he exclaimed with genuine anguish.

"No, he won't, honey," Missy consoled. "His mama will come for him just like I would come for you."

"But what if something big comes along and eats him before his mama shows up?"

"Well, Caleb," Missy reasoned, "he won't be happy if we keep him. He was born to be free."

"OK," Caleb said with resignation. "I'll stand guard then, behind the garage, and I'll make sure nothing gets him."

The Heart of the Man

"Son," Missy argued, "that could take hours! I think you should just let nature take its course and not worry about it."

Setting the bird gently in a thick tuft of grass, Caleb was quiet but determined. "I'll just watch over the little guy until his mom shows up."

Throughout her son's growing-up years, Missy could count on Caleb to bring in stray dogs, feed homeless cats, splint broken birds' wings, and free mice from traps. As compassionate as he was toward animals, Caleb's feelings ran still deeper where people were concerned.

One summer day, a few years later, Missy rounded the corner into their subdivision and noticed a little girl standing on the sidewalk beside her bike, tears streaming down her cheeks. With one hand the girl gripped her bike handle tightly. Her other hand alternately rubbed at her puffy eyes and clutched the shoulder of a boy who knelt beside her, head down. Missy recognized the familiar figure—it was Caleb. He appeared to be concentrating on the hem of the little girl's dress, holding it gingerly between his almost man-sized fingers. Missy pulled over.

"Caleb," she yelled from her car.

He turned to look. "Oh, hi, Mom."

"Caleb, what are you doing?" she asked with concern.

"I'm getting this little girl's dress untangled from her bike chain. She was going to a party, and her dress got stuck."

"Do you know who she is?" Missy asked.

"No, why?" Caleb responded, intent upon loosening the chain.

"I was just wondering how you got involved," she continued.

"I was driving by and saw her crying," he yelled back, this time without bothering to turn around. "I stopped to help her. Why, Mom?"

"Never mind, Caleb," she finished with a smile, rolling up her window and driving on. She had grown accustomed to catching Caleb in random acts of kindness. *How many high-school boys would care enough to stop and help a little girl they don't even know?* she wondered. *How many would even notice?*

The memories were running together now: the times Caleb showed up out of nowhere to help his dad mow the yard…the gracious "Thanks, Mom" after every meal…the late-night talks with siblings…the loyal friendship. Life had always been that way with Caleb. Incident after incident revealed a man of depth and character in the making.

Just before midnight, on the night after their discussion about sleeping on the couch, Missy slipped out of bed as quietly as she could. She had been lying there listening to her husband snore for nearly two hours, and her tension level had peaked. She had been stalling, hoping Caleb would go to bed before she budged, but at last she gave up. She simply had to get some rest. She had a tough day ahead. Her plane was scheduled to leave at 6:40 A.M., and she still had to prepare for a conference lecture. If she could slip past her son, he would never know she had slept on the couch again.

Missy tiptoed through the hallway, hoping Caleb wouldn't hear. She could see that the den light was still on. She crept quietly into the living room at the other end of the house and collapsed wearily onto the couch. Caleb was right; she didn't sleep well out here, but she didn't want him to know it. He was over six feet tall, so she knew he couldn't rest comfortably on the sofa. She dozed off but slept fitfully, worried that her son would find her out.

Then she had a groggy awareness of muscular arms lifting her gingerly off the couch. "Caleb!" she protested softly.

"Mom," he said, carrying her over the threshold of his room, "I told you, you're not sleeping on the couch as long as I'm around to prevent it."

"Son, I'm fine," she argued. "I was sound asleep."

"Whatever!" he said as he lowered her gently onto the bed.

"You need your rest too," she insisted, still whispering.

"Believe me," Caleb whispered, tucking in the blankets around her, "I'll sleep better knowing you're not out there. Besides, Mom, this is the least I can do after all those years when you tended to me in the middle of the night. Now go to sleep."

He turned, closing the door quietly as he left the room.

She nestled her face into the pillow and cried softly—tears of gratitude and joy. Her little boy had grown into a man and would soon leave home. Yet she felt comfort now at knowing that no matter what, no matter where or when, he would always be her beloved son.

Maturity

You can count on experiencing trouble and pain as long as you live on this earth. But take heart in knowing that nothing you'll face is too difficult for Me. I'm close to you when you're brokenhearted and crushed in spirit. I'll lead you to springs of living water and wipe away every tear from your eyes.

Tenderly,
Your Fountain of Life

—from John 16:33; Psalm 34:18;
Revelation 7:17; Psalm 36:9

Death is one of the most difficult things about life. When death happens in families, someone usually rises to the top and, by his support, frees the others to submerge themselves in the grieving process. That kind of selfless concern requires an uncommon strength of character, an unusual depth of perception. Families learn to depend on that kind of support, not necessarily stopping to consider where it's coming from, and rarely ever expressing appreciation.

You, my son, have been that strength in times of loss. You've shown me how to handle the hardest things through your courage, your determination, and your insistence upon going forward. You've stood in the face of sorrow and braved the passage to the other side while insisting on being fully alive. You have stood in the face of despair and chased away the fear. You've braved the deep waters of heartache and grief while carrying others safely to the shores of hope.

There is an unrelenting dimension of joy that characterizes your love. You infuse others with your energy, your contagious zest for life. And it has not gone unnoticed all these years. I have been the grateful recipient of your gracious gift.

Because you are my son, I have found greater purpose in living, greater fulfillment in every task, greater joy in the little things of life. You have blessed me with a deeper understanding of what it is to be fully alive.

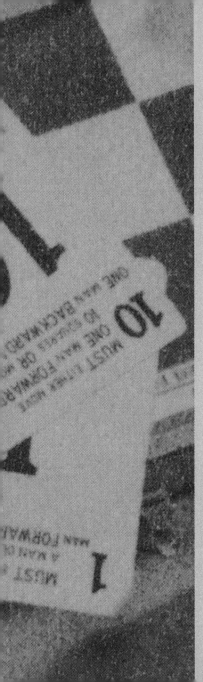

Cherish every
moment....
And hug
your kids
while you can.

■

James Dobson

*She recognized the welling
up of tears behind his eyes.
Only a mother would notice
the subtle changes
in his countenance.*

Emma Kaye's Sole Pallbearer

Kayla watched her son as he emerged from the limousine, unfolding his long limbs and assuming his full stature. Tugging mechanically at his suit coat, he approached the hearse. The door was gaping open, framing the tiny casket in a dark, dismal setting much like the landscape of his heart. He paused reverently, looking inside.

Kayla observed the features of his face soften—eyebrows arching slightly, the corners of his mouth wilting faintly—and she recognized the welling up of tender tears behind his expressive blue eyes, intensifying their depth and color. Only a mother would notice the subtle changes in his countenance.

CHAPTER SIX: MATURITY

Samuel politely motioned the funeral director aside as he reached into the back of the vehicle to retrieve the coffin that cradled his daughter, Emma Kaye.

Painfully cognizant that it would be the last time he would pick her up, he slid the tiny casket carefully to the edge of the platform. He lifted the sacred safe slowly into his embrace; all too aware that these would be the last steps he would take with her in his arms. Just as no one could help shoulder his grief, so Samuel would not be denied this privilege of being Emma Kaye's sole pallbearer.

Samuel went to his knees and placed the ivory-colored chest beside the grave. He wrapped his arms around it, and laying his face flat against its surface, sobbed quietly for a few moments longer, saying good-bye.

Kayla watched with deep respect and overwhelming heartache, stifling a sob that felt like a tidal wave of sorrow.

All Samuel had ever wanted was a family.

■

Emma Kaye had been born to Samuel and his wife, Jenna, on a sultry summer night in Louisiana. "Mom, we've got a girl!" Samuel had exclaimed, bursting through the doors of the delivery room, hugging Kayla in his robust way. "She's tiny, but she's a keeper!" he said, grinning and turning back toward the door where his wife and baby were being tended to in the neonatal intensive care unit. The sign over the door made Kayla nervous.

Emma was a mere three pounds at birth. Her tiny thighs were not quite the thickness of Samuel's forefinger. Her fingers were so fragile, they looked like the intricate detailing of a porcelain doll. Her skin looked so fair, so translucent, it was almost as though one might see right through her. *Her four older brothers were never so delicate*, Kayla thought.

The most remarkable thing was that Emma Kaye was a miniature replica of her father. All the finely-chiseled features of her face—her intricate ears, her pouting lips, her distinct little nose—all testified to a gene pool shared with the young man who stood gazing into the incubator that held the newest occupant of his heart.

What a blissful night that was, when Samuel believed Emma Kaye was here to stay.

CHAPTER SIX: MATURITY

"Samuel. Jenna." Dr. Simpson entered, his eyes pools of compassion. "There's a problem with Emma's lungs. We think we have it under control, but I must advise you that the condition is serious. We have her on a respirator. I'm sorry."

The menacing news of Emma's critical condition had an ominous effect on Samuel and Jenna. Samuel dialed Kayla on his cell phone. "Mom, you might want to come up here, the doctor has just told us that Emma isn't OK."

"What is it, son?" Kayla inquired.

"It's her lungs," Samuel answered. "She's not breathing on her own."

It took twenty agonizing minutes for Kayla to make the drive to the hospital, don the required surgical gown, and get through security in the NICU. As she approached Emma's high-tech crib, she could hear her son singing softly: *"Blue skies and rainbows and sunbeams from heaven…"*

He was leaning over her, singing into her ear. The song was barely a whisper, but loud enough to hear. Emma's heart rate slowed as he sang. It soothed her.

"Son," Kayla whispered when he finished, "what's the prognosis?"

"They don't know exactly, but there's definitely trouble," Samuel explained. "I know she's going to be fine, Mom. I just felt like you ought to be here."

Hour after hour, Samuel stood watch over Emma Kaye's little bed. Vigilant. Faithful. His gaze rarely left her. Kayla knew the infant had captured his heart.

Hours turned into days, and days into weeks. Samuel just kept singing and praying at Emma's bedside, hoping she could hang on until the worst had passed.

"Don't give up, Emma," he'd say softly in her ear. "Daddy's right here with you."

But the worst never passed.

On Monday, Emma's condition took a tragic turn. The mobile medical team accompanied her on an emergency flight to New Orleans, where the Tulane medical staff took over. Samuel and Jenna drove down with heavy but hopeful hearts. Procedure after procedure had failed, and Emma was weakening.

Late Friday afternoon, Jenna left the unit to make a phone call, leaving Samuel alone with Emma. There they were, the two of them, face to face. Silence surrounded father and daughter like a soft blanket, and Samuel leaned over the bed to look at his baby girl with no distractions for the first time in many days.

She seemed so frail, so feeble. He leaned closer, looking harder, realizing that his urgent hope had hindered his ability to see her—*really* see her.

She's lost weight, he thought to himself. He noticed that with each heaving breath, Emma labored. It slowly began to dawn on Samuel that every moment of her existence had been hard work. His heart sank with compassion and sorrow. He had been clinging to her so desperately that he hadn't considered that it might not be best for her to stay—that she might be too sick.

I'm her father, he thought. *She's depending on me to do what's best for her.*

Samuel prayed, but this time with a different perspective. "Father, I need wisdom. Please give me the courage to face what is best for Emma. I trust You with her, Lord."

He leaned closer to her. *"Blue skies and rainbows and sunbeams from heaven…"* he sang softly as his eyes filled with tears. He paused, committing to memory every feature of her face.

Emma Kaye's Sole Pallbearer

"Emma," he whispered into her tiny ear, his voice trembling with emotion, "if you want to go, you can. I understand." He kissed her delicate cheek and resumed his singing. *"I know that Jesus is well and alive today..."*

Emma's breathing stopped.

Samuel drew back, stunned. *She's gone!* He gasped. He stood there, staring in awe. For the first time since her birth, she appeared at rest. He glanced around for evidence of angels. *Was she just waiting for me to let her go?*

The look on Samuel's face clued Jenna in as soon as she entered the room. She ran into his arms.

"She went home, Jenna," Samuel said quietly. "Suddenly— just like that—our baby girl went home to the Father." They clung to each other, sobbing softly.

Kayla's phone rang at 4:27 P.M. "Mom," Samuel's voice seemed distant and faint, "Emma's gone home."

Kayla's breath caught in her throat.

"She died just minutes ago, and I'm holding her in my arms with no tubes, no wires," he said. "She isn't sick anymore, Mom," he said gently. "Jenna and I are saying goodbye. I'll tell you all about it when we get there."

CHAPTER SIX: MATURITY

Kayla was there waiting when they returned. Her son looked changed. Older, perhaps. Wiser. A weariness was etched in tiny lines by his eyes, but it was seasoned with a distinct tenderness. She'd seen him only four days ago, but he was different now. She held him in a long embrace.

■

Emma Kaye's funeral took place on Samuel's birthday.

What do you say to your son after he has buried his child? Kayla wondered as she drove to Samuel's house the day after the funeral. The image of him carrying that tiny casket was stamped indelibly into her memory. *I'm not sure what to do.* She turned into his driveway.

There he was, with his four sons—in the yard, playing football. They were laughing. It wasn't what she had expected, but the sight of him chased all anxiety from her heart.

He approached the car and opened her door. "Hi, Mom," he said, hugging her warmly.

"How's my boy?" she inquired, tears starting down her cheeks.

Emma Kaye's Sole Pallbearer

"I'm going to be fine," he assured her. "It'll take some time, I admit. But Mom, this morning when I got up, I knew in my heart that as sure as the sun had risen, so had Emma Kaye."

She nodded, still at a loss for words. As she reached to touch his face, tears now fully streaming, he finished: "In overcoming death, we must turn again to living. There's a lot here to live for, wouldn't you say?"

CHAPTER SEVEN

For Eternity

Make faithfulness and love your trademarks. Keep them as essential elements of your heart, and you'll win favor and a good name in My sight and in the eyes of others.

I've given you eternal life, and you'll never perish. No one can ever snatch you from My hand. May you fight the good fight, finishing the race of life as a fortress of faith.

Eternally,
Your Heavenly Father

—from Proverbs 3:3–4; John 10:28–29; 2 Timothy 4:7

My son, when I come to the end of my journey, I'll look back on our relationship as the crowning glory of my life.

I will recall hot summer days, watching my little boy run, bronze and barefoot, through the grass—chasing a ball, a butterfly, or the girl next door. I'll cherish the memory of a thousand frogs dangling, one at a time, from your chubby hands; fireflies blinking from captivity in a glass jelly jar; and dragonflies darting around your head as you dug worms from the flower bed.

I'll reminisce about chilly October evenings, watching you bound down sidewalks dressed as a goblin to trick-or-treat at the neighbors' doors—and to scare the girls dancing by as princesses and ballerinas.

I'll remember wintry days when, mitten-clad, you sculpted snowmen—a race of frosty giants standing staunchly in our yard, challenging the sun. You pummeled everything that moved with frosty torpedoes, defending your icy troops, championing your white battalion.

And I'll call to mind the warmth of springtime when you broke out the baseball cap, worn leather mitt, and grass-stained ball, rallying the neighbors for a sandlot match. I'll smile to think of you chasing the ice-cream truck or shimmying up trees and dangling from your knees.

But most of all, I'll bask in the joy of having known you from start to finish, inside and out, as my son. I've loved you from the beginning, and I'll love you forever.

Heroes build
bridges across
the silent chasms
that have kept
others lonely
and imprisoned
in their private
pain. By simply
listening, heroes
invite others to
share without
fear of rejection.

■

Larry Keefauver

*He wasn't a troublemaker,
but he was a handful,
his mother used to say.
Rose would add to that
that he was a heartful as well.*

Sugar, No Cream

After forty-six years, three months, and twenty-two days, the habit of sharing a cup of coffee every morning with the same man at precisely 6:15 came to an abrupt end for Rose McKinney. It wasn't intentional—the habit, that is. The cup of coffee, of course, was.

In order for two people to share a cup of coffee every morning, something intentional has to take place. Measure the grounds and the water into the percolator. Plug in the percolator. Wait for the perking to stop. Pour the coffee into a cup—two cups. Add sugar and cream, or not. But that ritual of sharing, day after day, year after year, throughout the entire course of one's marriage was something that might happen without planning. It did for Rose.

Each morning at precisely 6:15, Rose's husband strode into the kitchen, pulled his chair from its place at the table, and eased himself into it gracefully. Then he'd look warmly into his wife's eyes, smiling, and ask, "Where's my coffee, Rosie?" As if Rose wouldn't remember, after all these years, to pour his morning coffee. "Sugar, no cream," he would immediately add—as if she didn't know he preferred a little sugar, not quite a spoonful. And as if she would accidentally pour the cold, pale cream into his steaming black brew.

Each morning Rose smiled to herself when he said it: "Sugar, no cream." She mouthed the words as he spoke them.

She'd join him at the table with a cup of her own, and there they would sit, talking and laughing softly so as not to disrupt the gentle approach of the sun.

Truth was, McPherson McKinney—"Mac," Rose called him—was an old coot. But Rose enjoyed spending time with this man she'd married so long ago. He called her "Rosie" in the morning, over coffee. She sipping hers, and he gulping his.

Sugar, No Cream

Mac wasn't an old coot when they married. He was young and handsome, and he had loved adventure. Loved it so much, it seemed he was always in some kind of a "situation." That's what he would call it. One day it might be a conflict with a police officer over the speed at which he had been driving; the next, maybe an animated round of checkers with their son, Matt. Shouts of anguish followed by peals of laughter typified the father-son matches. Who would have thought a game of checkers could be so dynamic? But it was when Mac was playing.

He wasn't a troublemaker, but he was a handful, his mother used to say. Rose would add to that that he was a *heartful* as well. Rose loved her Mac—and Mac loved his Rosie.

The sudden end to Mac and Rose's morning ritual came when he got out of bed one morning, called, *"Rosie!"* in an uncharacteristically raspy voice—and fell over dead.

She had heard the dull thump of his body hitting the floor while she was pouring his coffee. Though she didn't realize then what she was hearing, the noise startled her, and she sloshed hot, brown liquid all over the countertop and across the back of her left hand before she could steady the pot enough to set it down.

Wiping her hand on her flannel nightgown, she turned and felt her blood rush hot and feverish into her face. Instinctively, and feeling panic rise, she ran into the bedroom just off the kitchen where she and Mac slept.

Where is he? Where did he go? She groped in the pre-dawn light, her eyes darting from one corner to the next. Suddenly she snapped to her senses and realized that Mac must be on the other side of the bed, out of sight.

Later she could barely remember the traumatic series of events. She tried to retell the story to the doctor, the police, and her son, but the details were tangled into knots of hard anguish and frayed with raw emotion.

She remembered pawing at him, rolling him over, trying to grasp what had happened. She was tapping his face tenderly but smartly with her hand and calling out, "Mac! Mac, it's me, Rosie." But the blank, expressionless stare in his eyes—a thing she had never seen in all those years of marriage—told her he was gone. Numbing denial swept over her senses and left her feeling paralyzed. Rose felt faint and helpless, unable to think.

Sugar, No Cream

Seconds later—though she felt like time and rational thought flowed like molasses—Rose yanked the phone from the nightstand and dialed 911. Holding Mac tightly in her embrace, she clung to his lifeless frame while she waited, breathing hard into the wrinkled, ruddy skin of his neck.

The coffee she had poured that morning turned cold and was later cleared away by some loving hand tending to the necessities of life after death has occurred—never realizing that with that brown liquid, something sacred was being poured out. Mac, too, was whisked away as other hands tried to resuscitate him; yet the precious cargo they carried would never again grace that threshold.

The last word from Mac McKinney's lips was, *"Rosie."* And the last act Rose McKinney performed for her beloved was to pour his morning coffee. It was a fitting end. But oh, how it hurt.

Had Rose considered how Mac would leave this life, she could have guessed it would be just that way—swift, clean, no-nonsense. Mac wouldn't make a fuss of dying. He didn't like it when things were mucked up with sensationalism and fanfare. He loved adventure, but he liked it sheer and straightforward.

CHAPTER SEVEN: FOR ETERNITY

Mac's funeral drew a typical small-town turnout—the church was packed, standing room only. Friends and family surrounded Rose as she stared into the casket of her dearest friend and only lover. Death has a way of being so cruel, so unfair. She hadn't gotten the chance to say good-bye.

The buzzing activity after a crisis has a way of holding off the harsh reality, quiet but inevitable, that looms ahead. Eventually, however, it shoves its way rudely into the morning and breaks upon the heart's horizon with a crushing blow.

The day after Mac was buried, that reality hit Rose. She reached for the percolator to pour her morning coffee. One cup stared up at her from the countertop. Not two. It seemed a mocking reminder, a finger of pain jabbing at her aching heart. One cup of coffee screamed silently at her, as if to say that there would be no more sharing for Rosie—not today…not any day. A torrent of tears rushed to her eyes and overflowed, streaming down her tired cheeks.

Slam!

Sugar, No Cream

Rose jumped as she heard the screen door smack the frame, ringing out like a gunshot. Then what seemed like familiar footsteps started, unabashed, across the parlor floor. Who in heaven's name would enter her house at this time of the morning? She glanced at the clock—6:15 A.M. Her heart caught in her throat.

"Hello? Who's there?" she queried cautiously as she moved slightly toward the doorway into the parlor.

"Mom, it's me!" a strong voice shot back.

That voice. The only voice like it on earth. Until five days ago, there had been two, but Mac's had been silenced by the fatal heart attack. This was the voice of her son. Mac's son. Their only child. Matt rounded the corner, looking every bit the image of his father.

As if he had done so every day for the past forty-six years, three months, and twenty-two days, Matt strode into the kitchen and pulled Mac's chair out from its place at the table. He eased into it gracefully, and looking affectionately into his mother's face, he smiled and asked, "Where's my coffee, Rosie?"

Rose bent over slightly and dabbed at her eyes with the

sleeve of her nightgown, instinctively trying to shelter her son from the evidence of her grief. But he knew.

"Sugar, no cream," he added.

She smiled and reached for another cup from the cupboard.

Through a gentle drizzle of tears, she joined Matt at the table. And there they sat, talking and laughing softly so as not to disrupt the gentle approach of the sun.